Author biography

Dennis Modestus Lyakurwa originated from the line of Kimwai. The blood continued to flow Through Kitengeso and finally to his line. He is a graduate Doctor of Medicine from Muhimbili University of Allied Health Services (MUHAS) and later he did a Master course of Science in Clinical Research at Kilimanjaro Christian Medical University College (KCMuCO). Throughout his carrier, he has contributed to the strengthening of public health. This time his tireless effort to support the community generously is beyond his plate. He has gathered data from different sources oral and written about the cultural history of Chaggas and narrated them in this book for the record, learning and keeping them for the next generations.

The author is a Chagga and possesses vast knowledge and experience of Chagga culture ~gained during his life and through his broad interactions and connections to Chaggas, he ultimately needs to revitalize and propagate the Chagga traditions from generation to generation.

The author recognizes that there are several publications which narrate the life of Chaggas from unique sources but he wanted to uncover some unintentionally forgotten traditional values.

CONTENTS

THE TALES OF THE CHAGGA

Customs and traditions of the Chagga people living on the slopes of the free standing mountain in the world. Their belief and the spirituality includes the mountain as the home of GOD

Dennis M. Lyakurwa

ISBN 978-93-5667-692-3
© Dennis M. Lyakurwa 2023

Published in India 2023 by Pencil

A brand of
One Point Six Technologies Pvt. Ltd.
Unit no. 26, Ground Floor, Building A1,
Wadala Truck Terminal Road,
Near Post Office, Antop Hill, Mumbai - 400037
E connect@thepencilapp.com
W www.thepencilapp.com

DISCLAIMER: *The opinions expressed in this book are those of the authors and do not purport to reflect the views of the Publisher.*

Foreword

The book contains exciting chapters, each with its own topic ranging from the chiefdom organisation system on the slopes of Mountain Kilimanjaro. The mountain is characterised to meet the needs of its people- food, home, climate and spirit. The life before the coming of the colonialists and the establishment of the colonial rule around the mountain. The customs and traditions of the people around the mountain are beautiful to keep- the relations, interactions, sharing, the art to solve problems, food and drinks. The ceremonies for newborns, marriage, circumcision, maturity and funerals are still happening. The kihamba is home garden is explained in this book. The first chapter is the introduction of the meaning and importance of culture to the Chagga people and the aim of the book. The second chapter is about the origins of the Chagga people, dialetics and the mangi system. Chapter three is a brief history and study of Mountain Kilimanjaro in relation to Chagga's life. The fourth chapter apprises the reader with knowledge and hand-on skill to practice Chagga customs and traditions. The last chapter of this book is the reflection of today's Chagga life, remaining cultural values and recommendations for improvement.

Preface

The slopes of Mountain Kilimanjaro maintain the provision to permit and commit life to the chaggas. Chaggas had married their culture. Their internal conflicts were resolved through physical battle, diplomacy and spiritual conduct. The problem began when the foreigners came. With her hand tied, the alien was irresistible. The last weapon was discretion. Some started running off with people from outside. Their culture has been stricken by grief and has indeed begun to despise their own. The traditions and customs of the land seem to be doomed. This book digs out the history of the Chaggas' life before and after the coming of foreigners to enlighten where Chagga slipped off before they fell. Also, the author provides some recommendations to address cultural conflicts.

The book is therefore written to display the underpinnings of people around Mountain Kilimanjaro, suggest realignment to restore our traditional cultures, the transformation of conscience and a genuine commitment to diversity to meet our demands and to interact with every gender, race, language and culture. Problems may be new but our cultural values – honesty, responsibility, kindness, empathy, determination and perseverance, generosity, respect, knowledge, wisdom and organization - are old.

The guidance on culture will protect men and women to inject their personal morality. The tensions and the suspicions from religions, education, media and other teachings can be carefully regulated through culture.

Acknowledgements

I would like to give my sincere thanks to everybody who contributed in collections of information and articulate them to the final material of this book.

Foremost my heart felt acknowledgement is to my family who prayed to me to the almighty Ruwa to give strength and power to continue devoting without losing hope.

The author would like to acknowledge the Late, His excellence Dr. President John Joseph Pombe Magufuli who recalled the importance of teaching the history to the new generations, in his speech at a national event during the swearing in of Ministers and Deputy Ministers on 9th December 2020. He said that Tanzanians need to know their history to become partriotic.

" Tunataka watoto wetu wafundishwe historia…ya Tanzania. Na hiyo ndiyo itasaidia kujenga uzalendo"

Introduction

The destruction of our future by the ignorance of the past in today's life claims us, a higher price. We can not reconstruct the past, but we can ruin our present and the future by forgetting about the past. Formerly said by Lewis that you can't go back and change the beginning but you can start where you are and change the end. The literacy of a society is built on the record of culture, ceremony, indigenous's knowledge, art, craft, music, political, history, practices concerning the natural environment, religious and scientific traditions, language, sports, food and drinks, calendar, traditional clothing, cyberculture in the digital world, and emerging new cultures which will become the heritage of the future.

The respect of people lies within oneself then to other people. It is therefore important to understand and respect people's social values as a resource than just opinions. They are the fundamental components articulated and sharpened time to time to make life possible. Chagga people extend their social values to the spirits of the deceased ancestors. Culture is the route to the root source of life through social values that bear us to one belonging; our Creator, The Almighty God. The highly discipline Chagga people differentiated themselves by age and sex to address their social conflicts within the same genealogy but mentoring and nurturing in groups and individuals using customs and taboos. Chagga demonstrated their culture during rituals in common and casual ceremonies; marriages, circumcision, funerals and through daily activities in their life. Chaggas enjoy excellent types of foods and drinks which made them exemplary health people. Chagga's culture have undergone multilineal evolution exhibiting new inventions and adaptions from outside. Despite external influence cultures discussed in this book survived and can be identified. Their cultural practice appeal to appease O men and Women ancenstors on both maternal and partenal side.

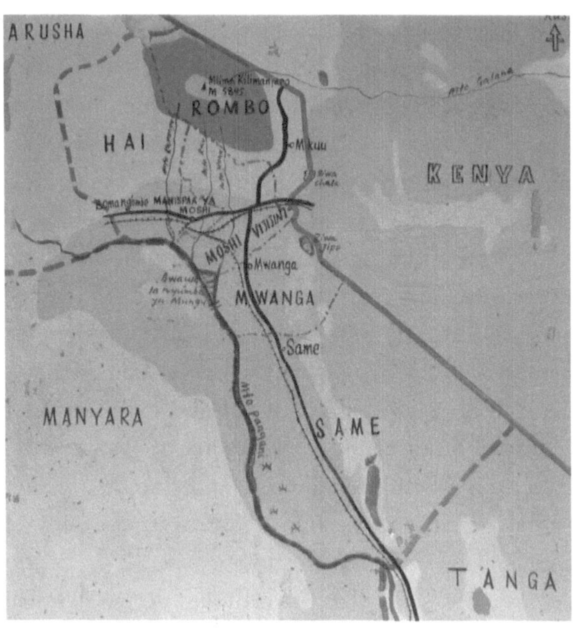

Chagga Organization System

Chagga is a Bantu-speaking people who originated from the Congo basin and arrived and settled on the Eastern, Central and Western slopes of Mountain Kilimanjaro from the 14th Century arriving in various hordes. Chagga tribe is formed by a heterogeneous troop from Sambaa, Pokomo, Dabida, Kisii, Taita, Galla, Kamba, Maasai, Pare, Nyamwezi and the people from Ngu hills (Christian 2017; Mhando and Mbeyale 2010). Group's movement continued even after settling on the foot of the mountain Kilimanjaro due to trade, settlement and raids. The dominant group expanded their territory by fusing with other groups through raids, intermarriages or diplomacy to form clans. The leader of the clan was known as Man-gi and was responsible to solve disputes, conducting spiritual rites and reigning people. Mangi had a system of parliamentary called Wachili which supported the Mangi to reign the clan. The clans grew bigger and expanded their area or shift to other areas. Mangi monarch system was a democratic ruling with a distinct judicial system. He rules over marital affairs, and land and family disputes. During the ruling, he gave each part freedom of speech to spit out the difference and utter all anger without interference. The Mangi keeps eye contact and remains calm to attend to his people fairly. He finally gives his final decision which everyone will have to obey. The Mangi connects his people to form the stronghold of a hard-working, patriotic and brave community. He oversees the ethical conduct of the Clan. Despite all tasks, Mangi did not demand higher pay. He accepted even a minimum reward of a portion of slaughtered meat, milk, local brew, women to marry and grains. Chagga leadership grew very strong and developed into chiefdoms which ultimately united to form a Chagga state in 1952. Chagga monarchy state lay from the Eastern part of Rongai to the Western part of Siha. Its ruler was known as the great Mangi (Mangi Mkuu). He possessed sovereign power over the state. Under him, there were the Chief representatives (Mangi Waitori) who supervised the Man-gis. Prior to the Tanganyika independence, within the Chagga state, the Chiefs representatives (Mangi Waitori) were; Petro Itosi Marealle of Vunjo, Thomas Mareale of Morang'u, Abdiel Shangali of Hai, Jackson Kitali of Kiwoso and James Selengia Kinabo of Rombo who was succeeded by John Maruma after his retire. Throughout the Chagga land, there were many smaller chiefs, and each of them was supervised by a particular Mangi Mwitori. Mangi Mwitoris and Mangis formed a supreme council that elects the great Mangi. In 1952 there was an election in which five Mangi Mwitoris; Ab-diel Shangali of Machame, Jackson Kitali of Old Moshi, Petro Marealle of Vunjo, Thomas Marealle of Morang'u and John Mruma of Rombo contested. Mangi of Morang'u (Thomas Mareale) won the election followed by Petro Marealle. On November 10th, 1952 thousands of Chaggas celebrated their initial annual Chagga Day. In 1953 Chagga Council founded Komya newspaper, which was replaced by Kusare in 1961 before it disappeared in 1968.

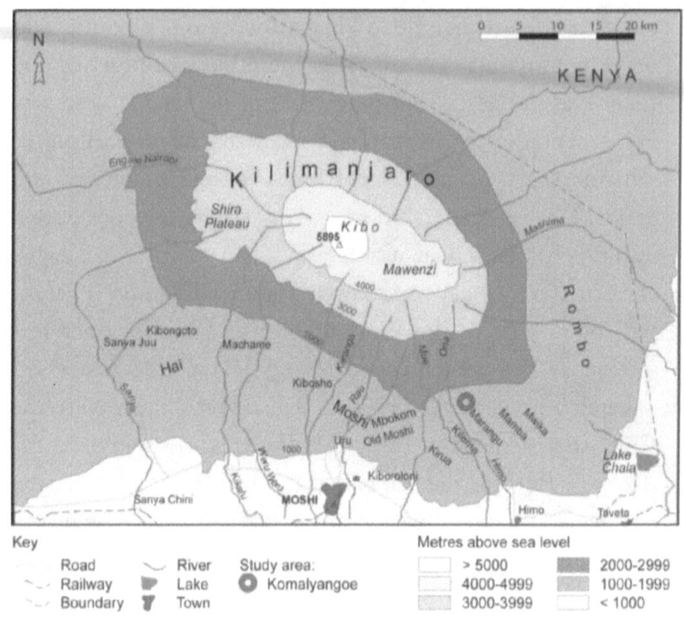

0 5 10 15 20 km
KENYA
N
Engare Nairobi
K i l i m a n j a r o
Shira Plateau
K i b o
5895
Mawenzi
4000
3000
R o m b o
Kibongoto
Sanya Juu
Machame
Hai
Kibosho
Moshi
Mbokom
Uru
Old Moshi
Kirua
Marangu
Kilema
Mamba
Mwika
Himo
1000
Kiboroloni
Sanya Chini
MOSHI
Lake Chala
Himo
Taveta
Key
Road   River   Study area:
Railway   Lake   Komalyangoe
Boundary   Town
Metres above sea level
> 5000   2000-2999
4000-4999   1000-1999
3000-3999   < 1000

Chagga Chiefdoms

In the first half of the twentieth century, there were about more than forty Chagga Chiefdoms. The major chiefdoms are explained in this chapter. The major chiefdoms are explained in this chapter.

OROMBO CHIEFDOM

Historical records describe the existence of seven generations before Ukonu. Uko-nu was the eminent elder in Keni who commanded his people to resist Mangi Marawiti of Mamba. Finally, they were subdued and Ukonu was made a vassal Chief of Shimbi. During the time of Ukonu Morang'u was under Ishosho and Mamba under the rule of Chief Rongoma. Orombo, a junior boy of Ukonu had uttered abusive expressions against the Mamba people. His father had forewarned him several times, but it was worthlessness. This created more tension and worsened the relationship between Mam-ba and Rombo people. After assuming his throne Orombo restlessly plotted several wars with his neighbours. The non-ending wars between Orombo and Rongoma of Mamba were settled by burring two virgins a boy and a girl in the Kishingonyi area. After the death of Rongoma Orombo became more relieved. He placed a wedge to fight Kirita the son of Rongoma who fled to Kilema. Orombo took a group of warriors and went further to the border of Morang'u to demand a Kirita's surrender but he was granted a refusal note. To express his anger, he killed sixty asses on the spot. Ishosho persuaded by Keenja came to fight Orombo in a fierce war that wiped out more than 200 of Orombo's soldiers. However, Orombo's urgent retaliation made them defeated and Ishosho was killed while Keenja escaped to Kirua. Thereafter Morang'u people presented Shamtembonyi, the fifth son of Kilewo as a vassal chief of Morang'u but later Orombo appointed Itosi, Shamtembonyi's elder who later allegedly murdered. In Mamba Orombo appointed Chief Kuwese as a vassal chief. After conquering Marangu Orombo went to capture Useri which was under Chief Kafuria who had resisted and fled to the forest, Overwhelmed submitted himself to Orombo.

Biography of Orombo

Orombo, the son of Ukonu was born in 1702 in the tiny obscure village of Keni in Eastern Kilimanjaro. His area of rule extended from Usseri to Kilema. Orombo was a warrior and the first chief of the Chagga rulers to attempt to build an empire on Kilimanjaro. Orombowas a physically strong giant of 8 feet and two inches. He was a person with an intellectual mind which enabled him to acquire skills fast, be courageous to battle the frontline and focus on his mission. His physical stature and mental capacity warranted him to build a strong army that went out to conquer all the chiefdoms in Eastern Kilimanjaro and in Vunjo from Mwika to River Nanga. At the peak of his rule his empire stretched over half the inhabited area of the mountain and today his name has remained as this district (Rombo), a portion of the empire he once controlled.

Orombo was born a twin and he was the second twin to Msangaro. Among other children, Orongo is a renowned elder brother of Orombo. According to the customs of the land, a second twin is usually killed. To avoid this, his mother hid him in a traditional crib and fed him until he was fourteen years old.Orombo was regarded as dangerous for his habit of attacking people and stealing during his earlier life. His father disowned him and wanted the boy hunted and killed. His mother pleaded with Orombo to return home and hide in a secret place. Soon after returning one day when he was in the Iburieni area, he saw an elephant eating peas. To be safe Orombo ran quickly and climbed a nearby tree where he hid on a trunk. The elephant searched around and no sooner it approached the Orombos hid. When reached the bottom of the tree, the elephant felt that someone was near. It lifted its trunk up toward Orombo. At this time Orombo already had known what the elephant is about to do, he then lifted his Panga and cut the elephant's trunk. The proboscidian went squirming and shuffling. Orombo kept his eye close to the biggest animal, and he could see how the elephant is running with difficulty and-finally it fell down near an area called Aleni. He went down and realized he had killed the stubborn beast. Orombo went directly to tell his father the story of killing an elephant. His father did not agree with the story as he knows from his experience how tough is to kill an elephant yet Orombo was just a child. Orombo went to tell the neighbours and relatives that he had killed the elephant that was eating the peas but his father did not agree. The neighbours and Orombo's relatives took him to the scene and prove. People rejoiced and shared the meat. They carried him up to the village singing.

"Orombo Orombo ukonuuee Orombo!". Chanting and dancing.

His father and the clan leaders gathered at a meeting and his father swore in Oromboas a new Mangi.

Later on, Orombo called his assistants and reminded them about the Masalue people who had chopped Orombo's elephant. His assistants did not know what the Mangi was up to, instead of answering they asked him what did he think of and he ordered them to collect cattle ransom. They went to beat them and raid their cattle and these Masalue people were shouting Aleni! Aleni!, meaning protects against. Hence, the name Allen was installed to date.

Thereafter Orombo went and told the people of Masalue that they were beaten because they had eaten the elephant that Orombo had killed. He ordered them to join him to raid Shimbi and offered them the booty to compensate for their cattle. He continued persuading Mkuu, Mashati, Useri, Mamba and Marangu. Orombo gave the captives and the war booty including cows, weapons, women and land to people who paid respect to him and he installed a vassal chief to protect his interest. His military strength grew stronger and fiercer than his enemies. Unfortunately, after his death, his empire collapsed and the region reverted to its former small separate chiefs. Orombo died in 1802 during a very fierce war with Maa-sai. After his death, Orombo's family was scattered. History tells Horongo escaped through Pare and settled in Morang'u.

MASHAMI CHIEFDOM
Mashami chiefdom lies on the South-Western slope of Mountain Kilimanjaro and it was the largest and most

populated chiefdom in Kilimanjaro. The ancient Mashami was formed by conquering other small tribes on the western slopes of Kilimanjaro, the Shira. In 1849 Mashami extended its territory through other Chagga areas. Its area covered the western part of Kibong'oto to Narumu, Kindi, Kombo, Lyamungo, Kibosho, and Kilema. Nothernwards to includes Uroki groove with a natural spring and a pool, then Mashami to the river Nanga while south-wards to the plains near river Kikafu at Nakukun the ancient tomb and Kiluletwa hot spring (Chemka natural spring). The wealth accumulated from slaves, ivory and weapons obtained from the trade with Swahili traders made Mashami very prosperous.

Chief Kivarya and his generation reigned Mashami and after him followed his son Nkombo, grandson Renguo and Renguo to his son Mankinka. Mankika ruled in 1861 and he was against the Europeans. In 1880 Sina invaded Mashami and took many cattle and women which impoverished it very much. In 1889 Mashami loosened its influence over other Chagga areas following attacks from Kibosho.

KYIWOSO CHIEFDOM

Kyiwoso chief dom extended from the East of the river Umbwe to the border of the river Nanga. Chief Ngaluma had exiled one young man who was against him. This was Sina meaning the borne breaker who came to live in Mangi Ndeserno of Mashami's farm. After the death of Chief Nga-luma Sina returned and briefly succeeded him. In his life, Sina formed an alliance with Waarushi who attached Mashami from the West and Sina at-tacking from the East. Sina dearly pretended to trick the death and retaliated an attack on Mashami warriors through a tactical hide and ambush. Sina overruled Mashami till 1889 when German forces penetrated to conclude the Chagga wars. Mangi Sina did not want a German mission in his territory nor wanted to conflict with them as he was terrified by their strengths. He unconditionally allowed them to establish a mission though cautioned his people not to support the construction of the mission so the mission was slowly accomplished. Germany brought more people from Zanzibari and Bagamoyo and in 1894 the mission was accomplished. Mangi Sina died in 1897 after he had allegedly been poisoned by his enemies. Sina was succeeded by his son who was executed by the Germans three years later. Sina's grandson, Mangi Sianga took over Kyiwoso, he accepted and pave the way for colonial establishment. This began the growth of Christianity and the establishment of the Kyiwoso missionary centre. A number of young Christians were brought from Kilema and Bagamoyo to form a Christian village. In 1898 Kyiwoso had a Christian-based education program boarding school and Joseph Kimalando was one of the Chagga boys from Kyiwoso enrolled on this program.

MORANG'U CHIEFDOM

Morang'u people originated from Taita, Kamba and Sambaa. The earliest known in history is Kilaweso the descendant of Muku who gave rise to Mtui, Mremi and Lyimo. The descendant of Lyimo, Iwite came to rule and was succeeded by his son Kile-wo. Kilewo had five sons: Silawe, Ishosho, Itosi, Nderima and Shamtembonyi. Silawe, Ishosho and Shamtembonyi were put to death. Kilewo was succeeded by Itosi and then by his son Ndaaliyo. After the death of Mangi Ndaalio, his brother Mangi Kinabo succeded him and expelled the wife of

Mangi Ndaalio and his two children Nderero Kilamia and Mlatie who went to live with Mangi of Kiruavunjo then to Mangi Rindi of Mochi and finally to Mangi Sina of Kyiwoso. Through wars of conquest (dynast) Mangi Sina came to defeat Mangi Kinabo and Nderero was placed to rule Morang'u on behalf of Mangi Sina. Mangi Nderero became renowned for his richness. Once visited by Masai warriors were excited about his farming bravery and they called him Meliari which means tireless. He was the first Afri-can to make a storey building in Morang'u. Mangi Nderero had 60 wives and died in 1916 at 70 years old, and he was succeeded by his son Joseph Mlang'a then to Petro Itosi Mareale his young brother.

MOCHI CHIEFDOM

The founder ruler of Mochi is Mangi Mandara also known as Mangi Rindi and originally his name was Makilo the ancestor of the Kimaro clan. He ruled Mochi from 1860 to 1891 before he was succeeded by his son Meli. Mangi Mandara remains an excellent diplomatic leader in his time. He handled the Germans and British relationship for the benefit of his people. Mangi Mandara sent his most skilled soldiers to meet the Kai-ser in Berlin and gave them ivories, minerals and leather to present to the Kaiser and in return asked for a few weapons. The Kaiser dispatched the soldiers with a music box and a sewing machine. Relentlessly, in 1879 Mangi Mandara sent a letter to the British missionaries the Church Missionary Society (CMS) who by then were situated in Mombasa, asking them to establish a school in Moshi. The CMS were very happy to receive this news, and they wanted him to become a lesson learnt for other local rulers. The CMS delayed implementing this request and Mangi Mandara had already given up. In 1885 two CMS missionaries, Edmundi Alexander Fitch and Joseph Alfred Wray went to Mochi and launch a station at Kitimbirihu near Mangi Mandara's boma, a place that came to be a German military station. Mangi Mandara was unhappy and threatened to close the station several times. Mangi Mandara did not want to cooperate and refused to allow his people to join this centre. This mission continued under threat and tension within Mochi until the establishment of the Germany East Africa Company. In 1891 Carl Peters was appointed as a German Imperial Commissioner in Mochi. Recognizing the intense opposition in Mochi, he shifted the station to Morang'u which was a very favourable place. Shortly after the shift of the station Mangi Mandara died and he was succeeded by his son, Meli. Mangi Meli took over from 1891 to 1900. His leadership ability created unity and solidarity among his people which enabled the Mochi chiefdom to succeed in a war against the Germans in 1892. German ordered the CMS to leave Mochi after they had suspected that the CMS was colluding with the Mochi people. In September 1892 CMS left Mochi with a few pupils to Tuweta. After the expelling of the CMS bishop, Tucker handed over the Kitimbirihu to the Leipzig Mission Society (LMS) on Christmas Day 1892. The first team; Traugott Pässler, Al-bin Böhme, Emil Müller, Gerhad Althaus and Robert Fassmann arrived nine months later and started their work at Kidia Mochi. Due to existing tensions, they decided to push westward and established a mission at Nkwarungo in Mashami. Gerhard Althaus established a centre at Mamba in 1894, and Robert Fassmann established a centre at Mochi in 1896. Mangi Meli became fiercer to German after resisting most of their operations. Germany captured Meli along with 18 other chiefs and hang them publically on the acacia tree on 2nd March 1900 at Tsuduni marketplace. After hanging them it was later noted that the Mangi Meli's heart was missing. His grandson, Isaria Anael Meli relentlessly requested the repatriation of his grandfather's heart until he succeeded in 2019. Bruno Gutmann (Wasawu o Wachaka - Grandfather of the Chagga) arrived in 1903 and was assigned to the Kidia station in the heart of central Kilimanjaro where he worked for 36 years, and he went back just after the outbreak of the second world war. In 1329 the Leipz mission had already opened seven churches in Tanganyika.

KILEMA CHIEFDOM

Kilema chiefdom lies to the west of Morang'u. River Ona marks a boundary between the two related chiefdoms. Mangi Mremi is known for his outstanding leadership and was the first ruler to formalize Kilema's chieftainship. Mremi originated from Morang'u. Oral history tells that his excellence was bountiful to the people of Kilema. Due to his generosity, He was allowed to settle at the top of Ngangu Hill and graze freely on their land. He was very much accepted due to his endless offering of meat and brew to the community. His good relationship with the people created a conducive environment for growth and development that amounted to his richness and prosperity. The coming of the colonialist found Pfumba, a generation of Chief Mremi, a ruler of Kilema. He played a very welcoming and accommodating host role.

Mountain Kilimanjaro

Hemp,1999, did an ethnobotanical study of Mt. Kilimanjaro that provided important information about Kilimanjaro Mountain. Important descriptions in this articles and others from oral historical information are narrated in this chapter. Kilimanjaro is the highest peak in Africa and the freestanding mountain in the world. This beautiful volcanic mountain lies three degrees below the equator. Its last significant eruptions occurred 360,000 years ago though minor volcanic activities were reported in 200 years ago. The mountain has three major peaks, namely; Kibo (5895m) the youngest, Mawenzi (5149m) and Shira (3962m) the oldest. In 1848 Johannes Rebmann was the first European to see it with his naked eyes, but there is no way his fellow Europeans could believe what he reported about such a characterized mountain. There is a good record of African expeditions to Kilimanjaro Mountain before the Europeans. Mangi Renguo and Sina had made many traditional trips to make rituals in Kilimanjaro before Oct 5th 1889 when Hans Meyer, Yoanas Kinyale Lauwo and Ludwig Purtscheller became the first team to reach the summit. The mountain provides life to all living organisms around it through its unique and wide ecosystem. It is a source of water from melted ice and rainfall that supports a variety of vegetation . Kilimanjaro is a spiritual home for

Ruwa (God) and it is believed to be the garden of the dead ancestor spirits who cast away all evils and dangers that may arise.

The foot of the mountain Kilimanjaro is suitable for farming. The rainy mountain forest just above the foot contains a vast of densely populated vegetation.

The shorter shrub less fertile area called the moorland heath zone is located in the up-lands after the forest. As one climbs up there is a dry desert also known as the Alpine Desert. The advice is to spend a little time in this area due to the harsh weather. From the desert one will reach the peak and at the top is the summit also called Uhuru Peak covered with ice and rocks. The higher the altitude the more oxygen tension is reduced and is almost halved at the peak which becomes difficult for animals and plants to survive.

During some winters there is even a little snow in the area near the base of the mountain. Notwithstanding in the middle of winter, there are days of intense sunshine with temperatures reaching into the seventies and eighties.

Chagga has two rainy-season climates. Hydrologists and meteorologists report hot and dry summer from April to November and a winter from December to March in Kilimanjaro. Chagga historical sources re-ports four climatic seasons; Rainy season (Asuma) from February to April which is characterised by heavy rains, cold, clouds, snow in some areas and green vegetation that favours the life cycle of many insects such as butterfly larvae (caterpillars). Cold season (Ksie) starts from May to August with persistent light rains and chilly. The hot season (Kwari) starts from September to November and the windy and hot season (Sisu) in December to January.

Many crops dry up in Sesu and there is a notable increase in house flies.

Chagga Chiefdom During Pre-colonial Period

The colonial invasion in the area of the mountain Kilimanjaro found Chaggas organizing themselves to create their self-independent state. Horombo was among the earliest Chagga leaders to unite different chiefdoms through the use of diplomacy and wars. Unfortunately, Horombo did not succeed due to a lack of governance skills. Mangi Sina of Kiwoso was more successful to establish a strong military system due to his experience in fighting many wars within the region. Prior to the colonial establishment, Mangi Sina had control over Mashami and Morang'u Chiefdoms. Mangi Rindi had won numerous wars before he was succeeded by his son, Meli, a famous diplomatic chief with higher negotiation skills. Meli de-feated Sina through a collaboration with the colonialist. His best negotiation skills enabled him to succeed in the different missions, but the colonialists had plans to eliminate him. Mangi Marealle forged a negotiation skill from Mangi Meli and used it to convince the Germans and later the British to establish and settle in Morang'u. His tactic made him greatly powerful and rich though he did not assume his role as a political leader over other territories perhaps he did not feel very strong as he won other chiefdoms through an oral mechanism.

Catholic missions were undoubtedly the first Christians to arrive in this equatorial region in 1890 and established its first centre at Kilema and expanded to other key parts.

The Establishment of the Europeans in Kilimanjaro

Before the arrival of the Europeans, Chaggas were trading with Swahili and Arab traders. These prominent traders spread Islam religion in Moshi, Mwanga, Same and Machame areas. The arrival and settlement of the Europeans on the highlands of Kilimanjaro is narrated by Bender, 2008 in the article entitled Holy Ghost in the Highlands: The Spiritans on Kilimanjaro, 1892-1953.

Explorers were the first European to set foot in Kilimanjaro. Rebman reached Kilimanjaro in 1848. In 1889 Hans Meyer and Ludwig Purtscheller landed in Kilimanjaro.The first Pentecostal church was established in Tanganyika in 1927 at Igale Mbeya. This was registered as Pentecostal Holiness Association.

Since then a considerable number of local churches and mosques are opened in the country.

The second group were missionaries. Fr. Anthony Horner is a renowned spiritan missionary who established a catholic society in Zanzibar. His work to evangelise Tanzania's mainland started in Bagamoyo on 16th July 1868. The Holy Ghost Fathers came to Kilimanjaro after they had established their station in Bagamoyo. On 18th

August 1890 Father Auguste Gommenger, Alexander Le Roy and Bishop Jean Marie de Courmont made a great journey. They reached Moshi after they had travelled for six weeks from Bagamoyo via Mombasa, Usambara and Pare mountains. Le Roy made a note of their first impression of Mountain Kilimanjaro.

"The spectacle that we have before our eyes are something that will remain unforgettable. Underneath a completely blue sky, there in front of us, we see the immense profile of the marvellous mountain. The two peaks [Kibo and Mawenzi] appear to be supported by this enormous pedestal…as a candelabra lit in the course of centuries to the glory of the Creator".

Accompanied by the German Com-mander Lt Arnold von Eltz the team visited Kyiwoso, Mashami, and Mochi and finally decided to settle in Kilema a place Johannes Rebman had reached. Kilema Chief ~Pfumba was very welcoming and offered the visitors, temporary housing and a place to build their mission. By March 1892, they had completed a temporary chapel and six additional buildings, as well as a furrow, to bring water directly to the mission. In 1910 the permanent church was completed. In 1892 the first school started to give education and skills to children necessary for learning Christianity, the children of Chief Pfumba and Mareale I, were enrolled at this centre too. In the same period, the German Leipzig Lutheran Mission arrived and the German Governor Hauptmann Kurt Johannes (The commander of the Schutztruppe on Kilimanjaro from 1892-April 1901) was eager to avoid violent conflict and rivalry among the missions. The resolution ended by dividing the area of the sphere. The Leipzig missionaries Southwest and the Ghost Fathers on the Southeast of the mountain Kilimanjaro.This provided the Congregation with both a framework for evangelization and also momentum, as areas left without a missionary presence could be taken by the other group. Between 1895 and 1915, the Congregation's presence spread rapidly, with new mission stations opening at Kiwoso in 1894, Mkuu Rombo in 1898, Uru in 1911, and Mashati Rombo in 1912. The first junior seminary, Saint James, started in 1923. In 1939, the first catholic Chagga priest, Alfonce Mtana, was ordained.

Chagga Customs and Traditions

The historical records of this book were gathered in Mashami, Morang'u, Vunjo, Mochi, Shira, Orombo, Kilema, Kyiwoso, Uru and Narumu in Kilimanjaro using a semi-structured questionnaire. This was followed by a verification of data using key informants who were selected on the basis of dialectics in Kilimanjaro. To explore specific cultural aspects, oral historical records and observations were recorded in Mengwe village. This village was selected purposefully to provide more insight into the cultural beliefs and practices in Chagga land. The interview was conducted by a native speaker (Nderiko Kitengeso).

The author is aware of some cultural variations in the group of the Chaggas sufficient to varying geographical locations, origins, lack of common socialization and conflicts among them. Though there are significant similarities across the whole Chagga land, the minor differences should not be ignored.

Mengwe Division

Mengwe Division comprises nine wards namely; Challa, Holili, Maida, Ngoyoni, Mamsera, Mengwe, Manda, Keni Aleni and Mengeni.

Mengwe village

Mengwe is one of the ancient villages in Rombo which is located between Mamsera, Manda and Ngoyoni wards.

Geographically the village is surrounded by Humba, Kitoo Hill and Marito Hills. The village's main road starts at a point that meets the main Tarakea-Moshi road. The road descends through Mengwe primary court and a police post. It then continues to meander and descend steeply from kinangura to Kiangeni and then crosses Kiungu-Mkuu middle road. The road de-press down to Kitimbiriu before it hikes up to Msasangeni. The road continues dipping until strikes Ngoyoni. Mengwe has remained a remarkable place for traditional learning Historical records account for boltholes and warriors found in this area.

Despite multiple wars in this place, people in this area had permanent settlements keeping cattle and farming collaboratively through Kyiendo, Uheesi and Kiarano. No wonder what we see today is a result of high discipline and good cooperation

They used to farm in teams. The harvest was stored in cribs for consumption and exchanged the surplus in trade with their neighbours. The wealth earned from the trade was utilized to build a chiefdom of Mengwe. History accounts for Wingia Ngache as a Chief of Keni Mriti Mengwe in 1961. Under him, Mangi Salema was a vassal chief. The courageous leadership of Chiefs and the elders expedited the culture to withstand external challenges and is set as a case study in this book.

The history of the Mengwe people began long ago. A man ascends from Taita hills the origin of the Eastern Arc Mountains. Kimwai is a renowned great ancestor of the land and the root of Horombo.

The oral history tells that the name Lya-kurwa and Kavishe started long ago. The two brothers were gathered to a hunted beast and asked what next they could do. The older said he wanted to eat it raw hence the name Kavishe from the word kavishi meaning 'raw' and the younger said he would drag it home, hence the name Lyakurwa from the word Kurwa meaning 'drag.' Kavishe kept livestock and Lyakurwa became a farmer. The major clans in Mengwe are Lyakurwas and Kavishes though these names do not necessarily indicate the origin from the same clan due to intermarriages and the second born of each sex named from the mother's side.

Traditional Pregnancy Care and Newborn Rituals

PREGNANCY CARE

Once married, the new mates expect a baby to assist them with small house activities; going shopping, collecting water and feeding cattle.

Across the Chagga, land pregnancy remains an earnest wish which will provoke the joy of the mother-in-law. She will start a whisper with other women about the remarkable progress and the expectation of her new Mwali. In a situation of no pregnancy efforts including herbs, rites, and instruction are performed and on condition that is not resolved a secret negotiation to invite a brother, usually from the same clan is encouraged.

Elder women motivate and counsel their parturient (Mlemwa) in preparation for delivery. Delivery was carried out on a near-home farm. Midwives were famous throughout the Chagga land. The mother-in-law and elder women are the birth attendants to facilitate the delivery by the experienced midwife. The delivery tools were; herbs, pieces of sheets, a knife, strings, a small bag (kkusha), a razor, a bowl, water, milk and a calabash (idivi).

Pregnant women fed on meals containing fat, meat, banana and millet.

The wife and the husband received instructions about labour.

It is customary for every delivered child to have a nurse (Mleri wa mwana), Later she becomes the junior mother of the child. The nurse is responsible for babysitting, feeding, cleaning, dressing and training the baby. The payment for the care nurse was a goat or a lamb.

The frequency of breastfeeding extends from 2 to 3 years unless the mother becomes pregnant again. A prolonged breast-ing was associated with the laziness of the child.

NEWBORN RITUALS

A newborn is a great blessing among chaggas. Chaggas perform a ritual to welcome the baby and to connect the child with the ancestors and the living people. The mother hides the baby inside the house where people can not see her. Even the father does not see the baby until he has completed this ritual in three days for a boy and four days for a girl. The elders conduct the ritual for the newborn. A male baby will have three pots while the female baby has four pots. On the first day, the women cook a pot of traditional peas with banana (Mbeere wa Mboma). On the second day, they prepare a pot of banana with milk (Kena). On the third day, there is gender distinction; for a male baby a pot of banana and meat and for a female baby, they make a pot of millet porridge with milk. A female baby has an additional fourth pot of ba-nana and meat. After the pots, they perform a ritual to remove smoke after staying inside for a while (Ifina Musu). In this ritual a pot of traditional peas with banana (Mbeere wa Mboma) is prepared, and accompanying children burn Ndeshi bananas and take the baby out for the first time after birth rituals. The woman roasts five yams, one small (unbranched) and one big (branched) and gives to the father. Now the father can touch and see the child after this ritual. The elder woman gives three yams to the sisters of the compound. On the same day, they prepare a pot of maize porridge and millet porridge to celebrate the baby out. The elders do not allow cleaning the baby by using water, instead, the elders smear the baby oil from the milk cow until he heals out heals the cord. After a month the baby necks become stable (Amevanga singo), then the father calls his offsprings (Vangari) and slaughter a goat to request more blessing and men mix the blood with ofal (Iveiya samu) for the nourishment of the mother. Give a boiled cow's milk for a low mother's milk. The elder women win the mother after three months. Start soft food (mashed banana with milk). The winning ceremony is characterized by a lot of charismatic greetings and givings (Naiomberwa). She is sent to cut grass and then to the market where she buys banana and sugar cane to offer people cheering her on the way. At home, she gives a present to her mother in-law who for the whole time has been looking at her baby (Mleri wa Mwana).

RECEIVING A BABY BORNS AWAY FROM HOME.
For a baby born away from home, it is the customs of the land to perform a welcoming ritual. The procedure starts by cutting a piece of skin from the goat's right ear (a male for a boy and a female goat for a girl) and the elder use it to smear a blood cross on the forehead of the baby. Then the baby is allowed to enter the house. The next day we finalize the ceremony by slaughtering the goat: a male for a boy and a female goat for a girl. In this ceremony family members and few neighbours are invited to enjoy the meat

and local brews. It is believed that the baby will run mad in case she doesn't belong to the family. and can be cured by his real father.For quite a long time this has been used as a DNA test for the paternity in Kilimanjaro.

Chagga Youth Coaching

A Chagga youth was coached to confront life from his/her creative mind translated into actions. Discipline and hardworking were major focuses for Chagga's early life coaching. Youths learnt to speak to the active hands, not to the mouth and to walk their speech and not speak their walk.

The elders once said. "Dumbu nkora na ila utankore na mateta" meaning mouth scorch me with food, don't burn me with defamatory words. Gossipers were (wandu ve ikimba) discouraged, challenged and credibly threatened most of the time. The source of information was important for the listener to transmit the message.

Youth learnt to collaborate and help each other in social harmony and heartfelt sorrow. They were stimulated to develop tools that will support society. Many Chagga youth teachings have been elaborated by Petro Itosi Mareale, 2002.

Poem about the hardworking Chagga by Dennis Lyakurwa

Title:MSHAKA NA IRUNDA

UBETI NAMBA 1
Shamesha Molisa, Safyaa mbaasa
Shaokya Motema, Ngafora vishaa

Ngausu Mareka, Nakawari ngaanwa
Ukame Maruva, Ngishekombya kena

UBETI NAMBA 2.
Ulesi Mbaaka, Runda wokfuma
Mlesi neshokya, kyamu kyerumbuta
Ndwali foileonekya, mtete ni irunda
Dumbu lakelya, mlesi mateta

UBETI NAMBA 3
Mrundi neshana, katema nefina
Katusa shima senywaa, sikafyaa sefumbuka
Shaa ya irunda, yefina mbaaka
Ndefo dunderunda, kyarano kyetema

MUST GET A BEATEN
In early life, Chagga parents and guardians nurtured their
children in a highly disciplined manner.
Do not greet the elders in the morning you are slapped
Do not greet visitors you are beaten.
Wash your hands before guests you are punched.
Crying for no reason you are threatened.
You get up while eating before the adults get up you are
chased.
The elders are sitting and you go and stand on the side you
are knocked.
Sit with the elders standing you are expelled.
Sent to the shop and come up late you are lashed.
Late getting home from school you are jabbed.
Cry for visitors once they leave, you are beaten.
Responding to elders in bad manners you're poked.
Insulting adults, children or peers you are thrashed.

When you are beaten, you cry, and you are stricken to silence.

When you are beaten you are silent, you are hammered to cry.

Beaten at school and go to talk at home, you are beaten.

Eat in the neighbour's house, and you are kicked.

Merely pass and do not get help from elders, you are hit.

Grasp something or hear a story in people's houses, and transfer it home you are stricken.

Choose the type of food to eat. You are pounded.

Play with strangers you are smashed.

The adult comes to sue you at home even if it is not true you are blown

Chagga Circumsion

Circumcision is the central rite of the Chagga people both physically and mentally. It is functionally the qualifying stage where youth becomes adults and responsible people in the community. In Chagga, it is customary to circumcise a boy after his puberty. Age-mate boys with their elder men set their journey to a secret camp away from home. Boys learn to become husbands, and fathers and study the security and defence tactics to fight enemies and guard society. Youth assimilates into their peer group the customs and taboos of the land. An uncircumcised man is traditionally regarded as a child and he is not allowed to attend some rituals. At his death, the circumcision ritual would precede the funeral rituals.

A boy sits on a cut banana trunk. One elder support from the back. The surgeon approaches from the front side and cut the foreskin using a sharp small knife. He then smears some herb and the boy is carried away to endure the pain in the hut. "You are a man, be brave and don't cry like a baby" This is an instruction from the elder man. The cut skin is thrown in the live-stock corral. After circumcision, the youth rotates three times or four times for a lady on the cooking stones (mashieni) as a reception ritual.

Singing: Waakya bora, Waava Msoro, Ukae sha Vasoro. Followed by Ululations (Ngulili)

The second ritual is to sit on top of the banana trunk three times (mboora) to in-spect for circumcision and smear butter. The skin of the prepuce will be shown to the father and his subordinate and then thrown into the livestock corral. Traditionally youths stayed for two to three weeks in the hut to heal.

After healing a weaning ritual was performed (Imishia mafwaa) for three days. A male goat is slaughtered for this ceremony. This ritual is performed using skin from the right forelimb and forehead from the goat all together to make a skin ring (kshonu). The boys wear an integument ring on the left ring finger and a necklace made of a small bone (about an inch) from the right fore and skin from the penice of the goat. To complete this adornment a circumcised man wears a traditional cloth (Mkololi). After this ritual, the boys stay locked inside the hut and they are not allowed to see a woman.

The third day of the weaning ritual. The elder removes the skin and the necklace and put them in the livestock corral (Msau). The youth carries a spear, stick and shield and begin their trek to the field. In the field, they learn to fight wild animals, and enemies and become warriors of the clan. In the field, you are supposed to slay an animal to show you are a hero.

Thereafter the youth returns the spear and the stick and places them on the roof. The circumcision ritual is now complete, and people gather to eat, drink and dance to cheer for the courageousness of the boys. The women drag the livestock dung and place it on the growing banana (it contains the foreskin, ring and necklace.). In the future, the first harvested banana will be used to prepare Mbege for the family and the stick will make a fire for burning the meat.

In the past women were also circumcised. During their initiation ceremony, the women elders teach them about marriage, how to care for children, appease bylaws and how to cook and work hard. The teaching was through instructions, practices, charts, proverbs and songs from the elders and experienced women.

Maturity Ceremony

WARI WA MRAMBO

Wari wa Mrambo means a brew to cleanse an individual and approve his adulthood.

This ritual is performed using brew, meat and millet porridge. People who have carried out this ritual can only participate.

Before the sun starts to set (just after the noon) an individual with his subordinate is locked inside the livestock corral (Msau). Nobody is allowed to see him until evening. Food and drinks are saved to the new adults on the traditional bowl (Irambo) below the curtain that closes the corral door. In the evening uncle (Vafije) and other elders dance and sing divinely to unlock the graduated adult. Then other people cheer to complete the ceremony.

Chagga Funeral Services

The death of a person is a great loss among the Chagga people. It is a physical separation with the beloved ones, it remains excruciating though spiritually still connected. Chaggas have distinctive funeral service that shows respect, recognition and love to ancestors, leaders and every soul. Elders would perform an additional ritual to seek harmony if the death was associated with conflicts or a curse. The number of rituals depends on the age and the extent of the family, whether married or have a grandchild.

UMBE/MBURU YE MSHIKYA

Umbe/Mburu ye Mshikya means A cow/goat for concealing a person

The first respect Chaggas shows to the deceased person precious is a burial service. For the death of an old man with grandchildren, a bull (Bung'a) is slaughtered, and he is wrapped with the skin before placed on the grave. In the same way, for an elderly woman, a female cow (Umbe ya Momaa) will be slaughtered. Other age groups are honoured merely using a male (Horo) or female goat (Mburu ya Momaa) depending on sex. It is contingent upon a capacity to offer a cow for slaughter. The animal for burying a person is equally recognized as (Mburu/Umbe yemshikya.) In the past Chagga were buried in the corral situated inside the hut, a place where calves are kept (Ookwa Mangashe) and a woman in the cooking place specifically at the place where calabash are stored (Ooho madivini, aka. Kshini). A grave was dug in customary fashion like a chair to allow the body to be placed in a sitting on standing with arms bent like a fetus in a womb. After maintaining the body then cow dung is brought to conceal him then add soil on top. After burying the dead person in the the same day, three bunches of banana special for ritual (Ndeshi) are cut without cleaving them (Maru ya Mmoosi). These bananas must be obtained from the same compound or close blood-related relatives. Other bananas are also cut to ripen for making Mbege. These bananas are sliced and ripen together with the three whole bunches. After they are rip-en, the three bunches of bananas will be cooked separately to make a brew for ritual while the other bananas will make a brew for the ceremony.

IOLAA KAA (IANUA MATANGA)

Iolaa kaa (Ianua matanga) means to cleanse the compound The third day following a death is a ceremony to cleanse the compound (ianua matanga , aka. iolla kaa). This day a bull and female goat is slaughtered, animal dung is burrowed and placed on one of the growing banana stems where the three whole bananas were cut.

WARI WE AYA NDUFA

Wari we aya ndufa means brew for sweep-ing the footprints The death of a child or person without family should be cleaned on the third day.

A sacrificial ritual is performed to humbly beg sorrow from the ancestors. The elders will plead with their ancestors.

"The owner of this home and the predecessor, Please!
This should not happen again, in case forgot to mention
any please know him.
In Chagga language
Monikvadho, Msongoru, Hai na Hai Ng'ndo ki
kitashefumya se kunu kaa ku. Kwa kolya kure mndu
ngamtumule no momanya.

WARI WA SENGESENGE

Wari wa Sengesenge means a Sengesenge brew
For the death of an elderly person, a male or female, there
is a special ceremony called Sengesenge. A male goat is
contributed by the grandchildren. In the presence of an old
man and a woman, the grandchildren are gathered to dance
around the house three times and around the grave three
times. Animal skin is placed on the compound and on it a
cooked traditional pea (Mboma). The usually caustic soda
is not put in the peas for this ceremony. The elder
grandson holds the end of the rope tied to the goat, and
the elder granddaughter holds the genitalia of the goat.
Each grandchild holds three pieces of sale and dance
round to complete three continuous rotations around the
house and three circles to the grave while singing.
Mmeku/Msheku ang'anaee............ Sengesengee
Mmeku/Msheku ang'anaee............ Sengesengee
Mmeku/Msheku ang'anaee............ Sengesengee
During the cultural movement around the house on the
compound, everyone takes the cooked peas and throws
some backwards above the head and eats some of them.
After dancing divinely the goat is slaughtered then each of
the grandchildren is given three pieces of meat wrapped
using the three pieces of sale they hard during dancing.
The next morning the pieces of sale and remaining borns

are collected and put on the same banana stem where the animal dung was placed during her burial.

WARI WOBULWA

Wari Wobulwa refers to a brew for spilling.

The traditional brew (Wari wobulwa) pre-pared just following the death of the person will be ready after one week. A pot placed on the ring made of four banana leaves and a wooden container is decorated using three banana leaves, all are placed on the corridor just after the door (Muongo, nekelawa Ksimbadini).On the same day, a ritual is performed to bring the dead person from his/her uncles (Imuende Kwa Vafi-je). In this ritual, the elderly uncle with his companion hauls a stone from his compound. The uncle heads directly to the grave and put it on the grave. At that point, he sits there with his familiar companion where he is given a bucket of traditional brew and meat from the hind limb (Nyama ya Uvaa) to eat and drink.

WARI WA MSASO

Wari wa Msaso means a brew for mixing the dead person with other ancestors

This ritual is typically performed one year after the death of the Chagga person to ethnically mix him/her with other ancestors (Msaso). Prepare a traditional brew for this occasion. Its amount depends on need and wealth. This ritual has a special millet preparation. Place three banana dry leaf sheaths (Mavidho) down one on top of the other to make a cross. Put banana leaf stealth (malau) followed by soft banana leaf (Unanda). Then pour millet and water and close the whole package (Maal-inga). Using a small stick piece the package to release water. Store the millet for a few days to germinate. Thereafter dry and grind the millet to make flour.

The second part of this ritual is during banana juice extraction as described in this book in the chapter for making mbege. Note that this method of extraction is common to all rituals. Carefully put the juice for ritual separate from the one for a general brew.

Pour the juicy for ritual into a pot (nungu) and a wooden container (iula) and place them at the compound. The next day pours the cooked millet porridge (Dika) and performs the major ritual. Soak the drinking guard until the brew spills over to bring the meaning of Msaso (mix). For a male, the ritual will start from the wooden container and end up on the pot while for a female the ritual will start with the pot and end up on the wooden container. During the soaking of the drinking guard, the elder utter some sacred words

"Mmeeku Shaamombe dwakfina rikeni ee, Usase na vameeku veengi

Uende na warini, Ataa vevekkaba ksido vekkaba seku

Utakumbwe se kunukaa ku, Dhuvaa dwaaksaksa na veengi"

Every person who enters the compound must pour three times from the pot and four times from the wooden container in case the deceased person was a man. In the event that the dead person was a woman then people will start to pour four times from the pot and three times from the wooden container. Every person is supposed to drink from the ritual before finding a seat. Thereafter people will continue drinking the other brew (Melesia) to solemnly celebrate the memorable occasion. The next day the clan members gather to finalise the ritual by spilling off the containers (Budhwa Ksumbi). For men, they will start with the wooden container and women will start with the pot.

The calculations are three for a man and four for a woman. Take a case of the death of a man, a man and a woman holding a wooden container together. Conduct a spilling demo three times and spill..x3 times. For the death of a woman, it is   4 times.

Thereafter, slaughter a bull and female goat or male goat and female goat to finalize the ritual. Distribute the meat as per Chagga traditions.

Uncles-Meat from the hind limb (Uvaa)

Sisters-Dhomu

Mother in-law-Meat from the back (Muongo)

WARI WA MENGELENI

Wari wa Mengeleni means a brew performed along the home pathway

Perform this ritual two years after the death of a man. It typically corresponds to male circumcision. This is a request to the beloved ancestor to continue to safeguard the family. Put a spear, a shield, a cap, a coat and a panga along the path-way entering the compound (Mengele). Prepare a brew similar to the one for Msaso and place it on the pathway. On the second day slaughter a bull at the path. This ritual means the dead person is willingly sent along the pathway. Distribute the prepared meat as per the traditional formula. Place the wrap of cloth of the dead man (Kiondo) on top of the cow's skin. Distribute the clothes to the grandsons of his familiar name (Vashuku va Rina lake). The first grandson is given the spear to give him a task to safeguard the compound as the dead man used to guard. Before starting to distribute the clothes, the unfinished bride price may be announced by the in-laws and can be negotiated. If not said presently it will never be said again.

MBURU YE MLUKWA

Mburu ye Mlukwa means a goat for raising the dead

The removal of the deceased person from the grave, three years after the death. One of the elders digs the grave using a small hoe and removes the bones (Irukwa). Tie the bones in their length using three Isale leaves and the cranium (Kborong) bone as separate. Take all the bones to the specific family place for collecting family bones (Mbooni). Place the bones; head to approach the Mountain Kilimanjaro while other bones are South of it (Iumba). Place a calabash of fresh brew and milk at Mbooni place. On the following day, elders inspect the brew and the milk. By virtue of the Mbooni ceremony, the brew and milk spillage or consumption has a reason. Under the normal offering, elders expect their ancestors to consume the supply. For this special harmony, it should not be abutted. Spillage or consumption of anything under no circumstances is a bad sign that no sooner person will die. The family members will have to perform a pleasing ritual. In this ritual slaughter a goat; place a few pieces of meat at Mbooni place and offer a prayer. The family members eat the meat and drink the brew near Mbooni place.

Chagga Spirituality

Before the coming of the aliens, Chagga naturally believed in one God (Ruwa) and the ancestor spirits. Prayers and rituals were conducted on the Mountain, river, lake, tree, road, farm, house and bush. There was a special clan and individuals to convene a prayer. Mangi led people to efficiently conduct spiritual rites. Traditional religion is traditionally linked to culture. It supports and teaches morals than disrupting them. It is real, practical and easy to understand; it was not recorded in any book but different people still practice it. Few prophets to mention in the prayer and thus easy to remember. Its objectives are specific; prayer for rain or funerals. It uses materials for facilitating the prayer: meat, clothes, plants, wooden utensils, pot, brew, milk and blood. Offer-ing is a leading part of the prayer. Money is not a part of the offering. The Chagga spirituality is a connection of living people, dead and Ruwa that communicates in different rituals. The Ruwa's power within humans unites people in sorrow and harmony. The punishment and blessing are awarded to remind people of Ruwa's presence and proximity. Everyone feared committing a sin because of the consequences that might happen to individuals and the community as a whole. Chaggas honoured God physically and spiritually with the purpose to see God after death, the punishment will be upon wrongdoers directly here on earth and they will not be able to see God.

The art of spirituality depends on the type of prayer but it includes; spilling, drinking, eating, spelling, silence, uttering, singing, apologising, commanding, requesting, gesturing, discussing stepping forward without looking behind. One of the elder men steps forward and performs the prayer with others observing quietly. The communication is to the spirits or Ruwa using the Chagga language. Women participate in the prayer by gathering near the house with their elders to drink and eat the meat as a support for the prayer put forward. Raymond Mosha, 2013 published an article entitled Spirituality Directions and African Directions Spirituality and John S. Mbiti,1999 an article African Religions and Philosophy, both narrated well how they viewed African spirituality in any context.

EFFECTS OF THE FOREIGN INVASION ON AFRICAN SPIRITUALITY

African spirituality was abandoned in some families, Some community members were discriminated against, threatened and killed, The Foreign religious teaching has a lot of foreign cultures which are not compatible with African culture, therefore difficult to follow. It caused a misunderstanding of the difference between God brought by foreigners and God of the land, Africans were forced to change their lifestyles for example from polygamous to monogamous without clear understanding, and people were forced to be led by a foreigner but historically, prayers are not assigned to foreigners. Foreign religions have higher demands for money, minerals and other valuable resources making them essentially business organizations. Instructions were given to larger groups while traditional prayers were for specific groups. Charles Dundas was the Moshi District Commissioner, and during his time he motivated people to grow coffee. People were happy with the economic improvement and they called him Wasaoye o Wa-Shaka. He made them believe him and it was easy for him to inject them with Western culture.

Slaughtering a Goat

In every Chagga people's home, there is a designated place for slaughtering animals. Women are forbidden to reach this place during the slaughtering. The choice of an animal to slaughter depends on the type of ritual. The selection is based on size, gender, parturition and quality.

The first ritual is performed just near the door (Ksimbadini). The elder takes a sip of milk with sale leaf and smears them near the back neck of the live ruminant, moving backwards and pronouncing words depending on the request brought to the ancestors. During the time of performing this ritual if another goat escapes then it will also be slaughtered. After the ritual, the bovid is brought by a man grasping its rope to the slaughtering place. It must be positioned to head Northway facing the Mountain Kilimanjaro. The goat is strangulated by one of the blood-related brothers until it dies. Chaggas confirm its death by ensuring it has thrown out limbs faster and stopped suddenly than one individual would test for eye reflex. The goat strangler would re-lease gradually to check his breathing. During the strangulation, if the goat makes the sound it is believed that people would die. To prevent death, the family members will need to cleanse the case by slaughtering another animal. The already slain animal is positioned in the same direction, stubbed on the kneck to collect blood after letting a bit spill on the ground for ancestors to consume first. The collected blood is stirred with salt and some milk to prevent clotting, warmed a little bit, add a little soup and fatty pieces of meat to make Kisusio also known as Mlaso.To prepare the goat for skinning the banana leaves are cut from ndeshi or Mnyengele but not Mlali. They are laid down to point north and in their position. Make sure you do not turn upside down. A dried ndeshi or mnyengele banana leaf middle stem is placed across the sternum halfway along its width to prevent stomach bites due to worrisome of people (ili mndu kadumbukwa nimo mutashevaywa ndeu.) This ritual is called Vatamana. It is time to remove the integument of the goat systematically following a tra-ditional formula. Starting at the middle of the sternum cut the and leave be-hind a small skin called ktodhoonda which would later be removed with a portion for the head of the compound (ikam-ba la mmeku). Then the whole outer layer is removed. After skinning Chagga retain local ways of inspecting the quality of meat. Cut the topmost part of a small banana plant and conceal it with a membrane taken merely beneath the stomach. In 2-5 minutes, the banana will grow to penetrate the mem-brane. In case of no growth then inearth the meat, sanitize and leave the abattoir.

Take a strip of soft meat (mrite) down-ward from the umbilicus to include the genitalia; the male is considered ngaawa and fe-male is ktaato. Following that, pull stake meat (taramu) along both thighs and remove it later with klata. At this time remove the limbs then the fore thighs. Get out the ikamba by cutting from the oesophagus down to the soft sternum and ribs joints up to the diaphragm. Separate an intestine by pulling the trachea down and advance the lumen aside. Trim a few pieces of meat from the oesophagus for ritual and the same from the liver. Cut a portion from the liver for cooking (Dhwasumbwa) for the animal keeper (Molisa), for the slaughter (Kmanya madu) and the remaining part is for the brothers (Mongari). Also cut the lungs for for cook-ing (Dhwasumbwa), for the animal keeper (Molisa), for the slaughter (Kmanya madu) and the remaining part is for the sisters (Vanamka).

Open the intestines and expose them carefully study to tell the fortunes and events within the family. The larger inten-stine (Mtambaliko) consists of ridges (pro-trusion) then the strangler's wife is pregnant and in case it has a notch (a deep one), no sooner a person in the family will die. The gall bladder becomes full of bile or the liv-er presents with bubbles, and there is significant rainfall. Family conflicts is denoted by the strands like cut lines in the liver. The small intestines burn on one side or the trachea has a notch means that in the family there are conflicts to settle. The larger intestines are longer than normal means there is success within the family.

Now separate the back by cutting the costae, starting from the inferior part, two ribs and the smaller one called keedhwa. Remove five ribs on each side for brothers (Mon-gari). Remove a part of the lungs left and the part of the trachea and its meat com-mitted (Dhoomu) for sisters. Detach the back for mother-in-law (Maamka). Cut the bone connecting the thigh and the back (Ilium, sacrum and pelvis) called Ksanga. Some of this bone is crushed and put in the blood (Ksanga kya samuni)

To take out the deeper parts of the whole structure turns down the portion. Get out Taramu and Klata and separate the Klata.

Then distribute meat as per the traditional formula;

Ikamba, and rumen (aya ya uwembe) for your father

Dhoomu and fore thigh (Mbadho) for sisters

Give Mongari the ribs; the elder takes ribs connected to itingo and the younger acquires ribs called mongari sa mualwa sitere itingo na isuru lyo lire maini yo.

The back, liver, intestine, rumen (aya ya kshoshi yo ire mfuko sha ktabu) and hind thigh (uvaa) is for mother in law.

Grandmother obtains klata, liver (iini la mo-lisa) , rumen and small intestine (iwa la kko)

The elders will eat the Ngasuma at the abattoir.

Distribute limbs to brothers; the goat lock-ers (mafunga mburu) and the goat un-blockers (mafutwa mburu) the part of bone after amputating the limbs. The head is for the strangler (Mofumba).

Kihamba

Kihamba is central and identity to Chagga. It is a banana grove in the upper land that surrounds a Chagga's home. In addition to banana it, contains trees, livestock, vegetables, yams, wheat, maize and fruits to provide a typical characteristic of mixed farming. Kiamba mixed farming offers an exceptional and best practice for a sustainable agroforest of mixed trees and annual crops to buffer the climate.

A chagga own a kiamba in the upper land (Mndeni) and a farm in the lower land (Mwai). In upper lands, there are a variety of plants such as Mringaringa, Modidi, Mkuyu, Mweresi and Mtarakua.

Chagga people grow different varieties of banana within the kiamba such as Kisukari, Kimalindi, Matoke, Mshare, Ndizi ng'ombe, Kitarasa, Nguve, Bungara, Mshare, Mshakova, Irongwe, Mkodosi and Ndizi Mzuzu.

The prominent animals in Kilimanjaro are Monkey (Ifuve), Elephant (Shofu) , buffalo (Mboo), antelope (Morini), rabbit (Mbongo), rhino (Mbulya), hyena(Sisi), snake (Shoka), giraffe (Ndweeka), leopard (Sisi cha Ngoe) and lion (Irung'o).

Other small animals are snail (Ikoru) , earthworm (Ishimbilili), centipede (Nda-laula), scorpion (Ksheshe), flying termites (Hong'a), frog (Ikododo), butterfly (Itandauli) and a bat (Ishaari). Jiggers (Mafinyo) and house flies (Masi) are known for their epidemic. There are birds such as wrens, dove, pigeon, horn-bill, eagles, duck, chicken, owl and cou-cal. A sound of an owl (Iunguru) indicates bad news of death. People fear owl. Coucal (Imodudu) attracts good luck. Small coucal ash will make you a fortune.

The low-er land grows long grass such as Balaang'a, Ng'arwe, and Ndikandika for building houses and feed cattles.There are bush fruits such as sourplum (Ndoloma), Sug-ar apple (matobetobe) and amarula (mng'aang'wa).

Banana Food

During the rainy season making a fire was troublesome as the woods are wet.

The morning starts with the crowing of the rooster as the timekeeper. The sunrise and the sound of birds and cattle provided a nice melody that keep souls happy. Early, in the morning, everyone runs towards the fireplace, at the three stone fireplaces the capitating wood is still scorching smoke through holes in the family hut.

To spark the flames, add some grass and small pieces of wood, when smoke in-crease blow it up with a fully pumped chick. Fail to light on the fire, people will laugh at you (Nonya mkoni). You may inhale some smoke that may cause irritation and transient cough with eyes reddened but don't bother. The fire will light on, and they are delighted and forget about what has just happened.

Mtango is a decent food prepared from banana and beans or pears with caustic soda. When the food is diluted with water become Mbeere. This is the most typical and abundant food in Kilimanjaro, and people consume it in all weather.

The beans in the boiling pot swim and jump inexhaustibly. Finally, they are tired and put off their shirt, which becomes their fate. They suffocate with water and become drowned. Mary Mother of God they are finished! they had known they would gather their energy and jump a big one to escape. No way! beans should have leant the mistake from the frog in the boiling pot, which waited and keeps regulating their body temperature until they are exhausted. The time for jumping is no more.

Add a cup of dark liquid slightly salty, lemonade, bitter with an aroma of spoiled water, this is a caustic soda.

It takes about ten minutes to start bloating foamy. The mother keeps her eyes closed as she knows it may erupt and spill off using a wooden big spoon (kliko) she squizzed on one side of the pot to drain the foamy and discharge into another container for about six to ten times until it ceases. Pill off and wash bananas to remove the slime. Put small seized pieces of banana into the cooking pot containing beans cover. Maintain the fire for about 20 minutes (you may check if you need to execute it more time.). Once is ready leave it to cool for 2 minutes and start to pound to soften it starting with bananas until they become soft. Then deep the spoon and pull up side to this side. Mtango is ready and can be saved hot or cold. To make Mbeere you need to dilute a small portion with an equivalent amount of cold water then can check if still need to sustain diluting.

Making Mbege

Cut and slice banana bunch into hands and keep them to ripe. Normally it takes seven days to ripe depending on the weather. Pill off and cook banana until it becomes light red (Water: banana 2:4). Prepare fermented millet (Millet: juice 1:4.). The second day add half the amount of water into the cooked banana (Dika).The third-day ex-tract banana juice (Tambwa). To extract banana juice take the soft banana leaves (nanda) from either Ndeshi or Shimbila types of banana. They merely emphasize not to take leaves from the Mlali type of banana. The soft banana leaves are taken three for a man or four for the woman ritual. A gradient filter is made by planting wooden sticks one-meter width to three meters long at three equal points on both sides. At the lower end of the gradient, dig a hole of about two feet width, length and depth. Place soft banana leaves to drain the banana juice into a container placed in the hole. Three along the path and three at the collection point for a man or four by four for a woman. In both sexes add one a soft leaf at the path and one at the collection point. Be precise to keep the calculations correct at the collection point. To minimize the speed of the flowing material for better filtration, place two pieces of banana stem intervals and grass along the pathway. Pour banana mixture at the first interval high up and a collection bucket on the hole. Draw the juicy using a drinking guard. The banana juice is called Nyalu. Cut a herbaceous plant flower and put it in the banana juice to facilitate fermentation, other people prefer msesewe or mokuta herbs for harnessing this process. Make sure you remove the foam that covers the top layer.

Cook millet porridge and keep it cool.

During the making of the porridge add a piece of hot charcoal to keep bad eyes away. In the late evening, the same day for extracting the juicy, pour a cooled millet stiff porridge into the banana juice and stir thoroughly (Ibala). Reserve half amount of a cooked starchy porridge for the same process the next morning. On the fourth day early in the morning uncovers the brew, pour the remaining stiff porridge stir it through-ly then the same day later just before the mid sunny people will start to rejoice and drink Mbege using drinking gourd (shori). Put some mbege in the pot that had stiff porridge to soften the hardened parts and make a typical mbege called ngorangora.

Mbege is used as a drink for ceremonies, solving disputes, praying to harness curses, disease, mischievous, mourning deaths, famine, relaxation and conversation.

Mbege is rich in minerals such as potassium-um, Iron and multivitamins such as Vitamin A, B6, C and D.

A well-prepared Mbege using clean and safe water is reported to decrease blood pressure, reduce risk of stroke, restore normal bowel activity, correct anaemia, lower cholesterol, improve kidney function, reduce hangover, prevent ulcers and heartburn and protect against neurodegenerative diseases. Though studies are needed to evaluate its safety.

In chagga customs, the father stays in a separate hut (mshalo). He uses this place for his own affairs, meeting with his wives relatives or visitors.

Breaking the Pot

This is a magic punishment. Breaking the pot was used to punish (Isesa) someone who steals or takes other people's property without consent. The magic finds (Sengeta) the responsible culprit. Usually, there are special people in designated clans for breaking and cleansing the pot. For example, we had the Malamsha clan at Humba Hill.

Procedure for breaking the pot

The first half starts early in the morning before people woke up. The Pot Breaker takes a hoe, gets out and hit it with another metal three times. dang'a dang'a. dang'a and states loudly "moofa" meaning you shall die, do the same in the evening and repeats the same for up to three days.Every moment after hitting and make a louder voice the Pot Breaker enters the house. On the fourth day The Pot Breaker wake up early as usual but this time naked. Then hit the hoe and states that "nungu yo isengete mndusho ang'iivia, isengete na mbare. Meaning let the pot scout the people who have stolen my property and let it reach his relatives and repeat it in the evening.

In the second half, the Pot Breaker hit the hoe naked for three days, morning and evening with an increase in the frequency of coming out and entering the house, three times for a man and four times for a woman (depending on the suspected thief). The pot will kill first the relatives of the thief for him to repent. It will kill more of them and the thief himself before it returns to the side of the person who broke the pot. When the thief re-pent procedure for cleansing starts. They slaughter two goats: a male and a female. Then they burn yams (Fikwa) and state that let this pot cool down. They use plants like ikengera la iduve, ibinu and mka-vaale.The pot curse might return back. The signs that it has returned are the drop of the ndeshi and mlali flowers (Naanwa). Sometimes, this would require more cleansing.

Rain Prayer

Plentiful rains in Asuma are associated with caterpillars (Fimambo) and other forms of insect larvae that damage plants. When it gets worse the elders perform rituals to appease the ancestors so that they cast out the larvae. Clan leaders slaughter a goat at its ritual site (Kliano). The procedure is to light a fire and perform the prayer. Many birds (Ngukuma and Ngooyo) appear and consume the larvae.

In case of flood, there is a clan for prayer (For example Malamsha). They go to the forest at a place called Kwa sondo to conduct a ritual. The procedure is to burn a banana (Nde-shi) and conduct the prayer and the rain ceases. In drought, they will slaughter a male lamb near Lake Challa. They eat the meat and throw the intestines in the lake. Without looking behind they blow the horn, dance and move back home. Rains follow them throughout. The next day they finalise this ritual at Klyaoni by slaughtering a female lamb and making a prayer

Chagga's Moral and Ethics

Chaggas have a deep, historical experience of the time aliens came in – while there was a strained relationship – foreigners introduced their butterflies– instil their wisdom - unconsented and without the will of the people. Finally, were dragged by the coercive power to form the Republic of Tanganyika

and succumbed to the drift of expansion, explosion and expulsion due to intrusions of foreign. The Chaggas today are fighting to heal their culture following the foreigner atrocity that left people dolorous.Many authors stated it clear that our history has been distorted. Here I will mention Godson Maanga in his article Rewriting Chagga History:Focus on Ethno-Anthropological Distortions and Misconceptions narrated clearly that foreigners read and feel they understand our culture from Europe but when they reach here it is different.This was also evidenced by Brunno Gutman who spent many year in the highland and wrote a book "Poetry and Thinking of the Chagga: Contributions to East African Ethnology that Chagga have good customs and traditions".After him Stahl, 1964 had the same insight.

MORAL GHOST
This refers to a loss of morality due to interruptions and mis inclusion of the morals in the children's coaching. due

to family, neighbours, education, or technology replacing the place for young children to receive lessons through instructions from caretakers, parents, guardians and elders. These custodians had time with their youth during daily interactions and in ceremonies like circumcision and marriage. Every community member was responsible to monitor and evaluate the behaviour of the children. Western education did not include moral studies in the education curriculum though it grabbed our children from home for many hours with strangers at school. The characters of children bet on the home environment which is predominantly determined by the parents/guardians' care. Their integrity depends on their parents/guardians and their community. The reflection of children's characters is determined by parents/guardians' warmth and affection for each other, acting in a civilized way, respecting elders, loving juniors and politeness in conversation. A society with better moral practices remains stronger and united and leaves behind a good reputation. After political independence, the African governments suffered economic instability due to a lack of capital and plans for a sustainable economy fueled by government demand and expenses to meet the need of the growing population and changes in technology. This intensified an economic burden on its people. The interference in the economic activities of people increases corruption and crimes which continue to erode the morals of society.

Good technology improves physical, social, medical, psychological, spiritual, and moral. It helps people to become healthier, more creative and innovative, more educated, more loving of God and neighbour, and better at making moral decisions. Bad technology will harm our life:

take our time, misinform us, make us lazier, creates poor health, causes conflict and wars, increases crimes and erode our morals.

Once Peter Maurin, a founder of the Catholic Worker Movement said "The world would be better off if people tried to become better"

Social networks such as WhatsApp, Facebook, Instagram, Twitter, Flickr, YouTube, Qzone, Weibo, LinkedIn, Reddit, Pinterest VK, Odnoklassniki and Tumbir are as good as they were made for. Together with these social networks other tools that create community interaction are televisions, radios, magazines, computers, the internet, sports, games, movies, music and mobile phones. Operate on a wide geographic area that essentially has different cultures. Share knowledge and experience from different places. Connect people and institutions working on various topics or agendas. Spread love and affection. Source of income for people who sell their products. Mention inexhaustibly. Bad people use the same channels to spread false information, terror and fear. Allure people's attention and emotions and make them dependent on these media. Steal time. Mix cultures and erode morals by branding the bad things and under or misreporting the better values. Teach youth how to misbehave, disrespect the elders and commit sins. Relay information from different places that can cause confusion, depression, sleep and digestive problems to the individual.

Throw messages vagrantly without the consent of the receivers on topics or materials. Consume people's money in form of airtime bundles.

MORAL RECAPITULATION

Moral values eventually develop the ethics of society. Below are some of the important and recommendable ethical principles for the Chagga.

HONESTY

Currently, people on social digital media tell lies about their location, deceive on time and try to hide their identity for personal gain. In the past once committed a crime a Chagga would admit and pay an excuse for the wrong done. A fine was charged as compensation for dishonesty. The amount of fine depended on the size of the crime. Some crimes amounted to a death or being exiled out of the territory.

RESPONSIBILITY

Have you heard several parents complaining about their children's laziness, that they are very much confined to the sitting room watching TV and playing games? In the past, Chagga youth learnt to become responsible in their life. Youth helped their parents fetch water, collect firewood, farm, cook and feed animals. Apart from this, they had their small projects like making and selling sisal ropes, selling avocados keeping rabbits and hens which gave them funds to buy their requirements. Children depended on themselves in buying clothes, books and pens.

KINDNESS

According to customs, Chagga lived in their Kiamba helping each other with food, water, sickness and work. They worked cooperatively to make their houses, dig farms and harvest crops.

EMPATHY

In situations of accident or disease, people gather to help each other. A cry for help (Ufuo) attracted people to provide assistance as quickly as possible. Funerals are attended by the majority and none want to miss the occasion. Empathy among Chaggas has been well maintained.

DETERMINATION AND PERSEVERANCE

Chaggas set goals, fervently believe, vigorously act, and fix their gaze to determine reality. They did not quit easily no matter how hard things get, they keep on finding what works and what doesn't and dedicate countless hours of their time without losing hope.

GENEROSITY

Chaggas are generous by nature. Foods and drinks are shared. Though scarce and expensive Chaggas continue to share food and drinks as tools for diplomacy, peace and prestige. The offering to people is storing for yourself.

RESPECT

Chaggas maintained respect for elders, people with abilities, qualities and achievements are treated with honour.

TRAINING AND MENTORING

Chagga parents, guardians and elders mentored and trained the youth on discipline and hardworking. The grandparents had a special role in nurturing the youth after their puberty.

ORGANIZATION SYSTEM

Chaggas had a strong Mangi system that coordinated the security, governed, oversees and connected people to God.

Chagga's Life Today

Currently, Chaggas start their day early morning and work an English five-day week, with two days Saturday and Sunday off.

Schools operate the same with the day starting early and ending in the early evening for most children. The younger children finish their studies around noon and the older children finish classes around the evening or otherwise, they stay in boarding schools. As a result of a busy schedule, most Chagga homes require a caretaker to serve the younger kids their main meal in the early afternoon. Social evenings or weekends are tight and mixed with discussions for opportunities, drinking and making deals, in which children are automatically excluded.

The cost of living in Kilimanjaro is relatively cheaper than in Western countries. Most Chagga housewives go shopping in community markets or supermarkets daily as they prefer fresh foods to refrigerated feed. Meat is one of the favourite food among the Chagga (a kilo of raw beef costs $3.50). A local hen ($8.5.00 per one) and a broiler ($4.5.00 per one). A kilo of a local fresh-water tilapia ($6.00). A smoked or fried small Tilapia (a bunch of three or four for $ 1.00), vegetables 0.25$ and a litre of sour or fresh milk are $ 0.50, a budget-minded family will prefer dried fish and vegetables to keep the food expenses down. Every purchase in Kilimanjaro is by Cash (No credit cards) and people can afford it. Housing is abundant and family-owned single-type dwellings are available for the visitors as homestays where they share the same compound with the family. The apartments are numerous and most rooms are standard with televisions, radios, internet and mobile phone services available. Hotels for visitors who need private and luxurious moments are plenty and also affordable. Security surveillance in Kilimanjaro is performed by the community and the government security systems. Chagga continues enjoying marriage, newborn, circumcision and funeral ceremonies mixed with foreign celebrations such as birthdays, engagement, communion, confirmation and others.

Recommendations

This book is a collection of oral and written documents about the Cultural History of Chaggas. There are good values that Chaggas practised, still practices or will need to reinstall them. This anthropological book is written to reconstruct the history of the land and I have listed my recommendations here down;

I recommend anyone proven to conduct dishonestly s/he should admit, pay excuse and a goat for the wrong done.

I suggest to a Chagga youth 12 years and above should run a short project to earn and save in a bank account a minimum of Tsh. 1000,000/= per year. The amount to be reviewed from time to time depends on the capacity.

Chagga people are encouraged to form as many community organisations as cooperatives or other registered groups, participate actively and pay contributions on time. Through these organisations, the customs to help each other shall heal.

It is emphasized that Chaggas should continue to attend social gatherings and support each other in sorrow and harmony. Funerals and ceremonies are important social values.

Chaggas are advised to set goals, keep a focus, track, and review what works or not works constantly without losing hope.

Chaggas are encouraged to continue their generosity.

Chagga people should continue to respect elders and people who have worked and achieved well.

Chaggas are advised to set some time for their children and appoint cultural teachers who can support them. Design a -one-month cultural curriculum to train the youth during their holidays. Every Chagga youth should pass the one-month cultural training once in their lifetime and receive a certificate. Chagga cultural leaders are advised to team up to develop a curriculum for cultural training that will be incorporated into the education system.

Chaggas are advised to use technology wisely for their development and to document and preserve their cultural values. The material that is used or exacerbates falsifiers, disruptors, procrastinators, and moral traitors should be perpetually condemned and pacified.

I appeal to reinstall the Mangi system which will supervise the cultural values of the Chaggas. Mangis can be selected from every Administrative Division. The qualification for this position includes but is not limited to the capacity to reign, commitment, experience and history of the clan, the ancestors of an individual. These Mangis shall be able to recall the customs and traditions of the land without interfering with the Tanzanian constitution, laws and regulations. The Mangis shall select the Mangi Mkuu as the chief cultural superintendent and the head of the traditional religion. Revive the Chagga Day of 10th November and commemorate it with all diligence.

This is the time to appease and recall our ancestor's spirits; keep our better history; and carry our culture forward from generation to generation as our covenant.

Appendix

KIWOSO

Kiwoso originates from Buntu language... ... explaination
.... In the appendix an overview of all relevant greetings
and voicabulary table is included.

Morning greeting

Nanto mbe or saa/ma/kyoo/kyekuu –meaning: Good
morning fa-ther/mother/grandfather/grandmother.

Reply-Eka mbe or saa/ma/kyoo/kyekuu-meaning: Thanks
fa-ther/mother/grandfather/grandmother.A short reply:ne
ewe kwanto!-meaning:Goodmorning to you too.

Afternoon greeting

Nasindiso mbe or saa/ma/kyoo/kyekuu –meaning: Good
afternoon fa-ther/mother/grandfather/grandmother.

Reply-Eka mbe or saa/ma/kyoo/kyekuu-meaning: Thanks
fa-ther/mother/grandfather/grandmother.A short reply:ne
ewe kwanto!-meaning:Good afternoon to you too.

How have you been?

Kuifo kuda mbe or saa/ma/kyoo/kyekuu –meaning: how
have you been fa-ther/mother/grandfather/grandmother.

Reply-ngiifo nicha mbe or saa/ma/kyoo/kyekuu-meaning:
I'm good fa-ther/mother/grandfather/grandmother.

Congratulation for a good work

Kocha   mbe   or   saa/ma/kyoo/kyekuu   –meaning:
congratulation   for   a   good   work   fa-
ther/mother/grandfather/grandmother.

Reply-eka mbe or saa/ma/kyoo/kyekuu-meaning: Thanks fa-ther/mother/grandfather/grandmother.
How are you? (For people of the same age)
nkida –meaning: how are you .
Reply-nkido tubu -meaning: I'm good.

KIOROMBO

Morning greeting
Sha waamka /Waamka /Umeamka baba or mbe or aba or papa   or lai or tata/mama or mani or mai / mmeku/msheku or vatoi / avae or vaita/mshiki.
Meaning   -Good   morning father/mother/grandfather/grand mother/brother/sister
After noon greeting
Umesinda/Wasinda   baba or aba or mbe papa or lai or tata/mama or mani or mai / mmeku/msheku or vatoi /avae or vaita/mshiki. Meaning -Good afternoon father/mother/grandfather/grand mother/brother/sister
Congratulation for a good work (1)
Umetana /Watana baba or mbe or aba or papa or lai or tata/mama or mani or mai / mmeku/msheku or vatoi / avae   or   vaita/mshiki.   Meaning   -congratulation father/mother/grandfather/grand mother/brother/sister
Congratulation for a good work (2)
Naksha waookya/umeokya/Sha waokya baba or mbe or aba or papa or lai or tata/mama or mani or mai / mmeku/msheku or vatoi /avae or vaita/mshiki. Meaning - congratulation   father/mother/grandfather/grand mother/brother/sister
Congratulation for a good work (3)
Shamesha baba or mbe or aba or papa or lai or tata/mama or mani or mai / mmeku/msheku or vatoi /avae or

vaita/mshiki. Meaning -Congratulation father/mother/grandfather/grand mother/brother/sister

Night greetings

Kokyamse or Kulae or kwelala or namatio baba or mbe or aba or papa or lai or tata/mama or mani or mai / mmeku/msheku or vatoi /avae or vaita/mshiki. Meaning - Good night father/mother/grandfather/grand mother/brother/sister

KIMORANG'U

Morning greeting

Kamsa mbe/mae/mbe/mai/awae/mshiki =Good morning fa-ther/mother/grandfather/grandmother

Reply- Kapfo monoko/mchuku/awae/msacha/mshiki

Meaning: Good morning to you my child/ grandchild/elder/brother/sister

Afternoon greeting

Kosinda mbe or /mae/mbe/mae =Good afternoon fa-ther/mother/grandfather/grandmother

Reply- Aika monoko/mchuku/awae/msacha/mshiki

Meaning: Thanks my child/ grandchild/elder/brother/sister

Otana mbe/mae/mbe/mae =Congratulation for good work fa-ther/mother/grandfather/grandmother

Reply- Aika monoko/mchuku/awae/msacha/mshiki

Meaning: Thanks my child/ grandchild/elder/brother/sister

How are you?

Shimbonyi

Shimbonyi Shapfo

Shimbonyi sha ngamenyi.-meaning Good morning.Shimbonyi sha

awuyo/momo/asauyo/akyekuyo/wowoo/mananyu —
meaning how is your father/mother/grand
father/grandmother/ elder brother or sister/young
brother or sister (Usually this salute is given by an elder to
a younger or people of the same age. Young people can not
give this to their elders).
Reply1 –Naashicha ,kapisa,aika ,ungiwie shapfo.
Reply 2-Ngiimcha kapisa
Night greetings
Kulale .Meaning Good night
Reply- Kapfo monoko/mchuku/awae/msacha/mshiki
Meaning: Thanks my child/
grandchild/elder/brother/sister
NB: In marangu Morning is ngamenyi, afternoon is
kyingoto, evening is kyiukonyi and night is kyio.

KIMASHAMI
Morning greetings
Naantwa (Good morning)
Wakubo foenda (Good morning to you. Usually this salute
is given by an elder to a younger or people of the same age.
Young people can not give this to their elders)
Naantwa mae or mbee/ma/ /mmiku/nkyeku/
nsero/mankya
Meaning-Good morning father/mother
/grandfather/grandmother/brother/sister.
Reply through age and gender classification (1)
Reply Eka mae or mbee/ama/ /mmiku/nkyeku/
nsero/mankya
Reply can be done using a clan name (2) eg.Eka mae
Ndosi, Eka mae Kileo, Eka mankya.
Kuifoeenda mae or mbee/ama/ /mmiku/nkyeku/

nsero/mankya.

Reply-(I'm good= Eka mae or mbee/ama/ /mmiku/nkyeku/ nsero/mankya)

After noon greatings

Nasindiswa mae or mbee/ama/ /mmiku/nkyeku/ nsero/mankya

Reply -Eka mae or mbee/ama/ /mmiku/nkyeku/ nsero/mankya meaning-Thanks (Mentioned the gender or family name)

How are you?

Nyindaro mae or mbee/ama/ /mmiku/nkyeku/ nsero/mankya

Reply-(I'm good= Eka mae or mbee/ama/ /mmiku/nkyeku/ nsero/mankya)

Kuifoeenda (one)

Mwifoeenda ini (many) .

Mbontafoo? Reply-(I'm good= Eka mae or mbee/ama/ /mmiku/nkyeku/ nsero/mankya)

Congratulation for a good work

Kololya mae or mbee/ama/ /mmiku/nkyeku/ nsero/mankya

Eka Nkeeku/Mbe/Ma

How have you been

Sisa mae or mbee/ama/ /mmiku/nkyeku/ nsero/mankya

Kusinde na ufoo mae or mbee/ama/ /mmiku/nkyeku/ nsero/mankya

Eka Nkeeku/Mbe/Ma

KIURU

Morning greeting

Kwamza mbee /maee/mbee/maee/saa –meaning: Good morning fa-ther/mother/ /grandfather/grandmother/the

second male born
Reply-Naiyo mbee /maee/kekuu/saa
Shimboni shafoo mbee/maee
Reply Shicha mbee/maee/saa/ngoe
Usually this salute is given by agemates. Young people can not give this to their elders.
Afternoon greeting
Zindangoto   mbee/maee/mbee/maee–meaning: Good afternoon fa-ther/mother/grandfather/grandmother.
Repy Shicha tupu mbe/mae
Congratulation for a good work
Kocha mbee/mae/saa/ngoe/
Reply Aika mbe/mae/saa/ngoe
–meaning: congratulation for a good work fa-ther/mother/grandfather/grandmother/brother/sister
Night greeting
Lalakucha mbee/maee/ngoe
meaning: Good night?.
Reply- Aika mbe/mae
-meaning: Thanks.
NB: In URU morning is Otuko, afternoon is kingoto, evening is kikwanyi and night is kyio.

KISHIRA
Morning greeting
Kwanto ahee (Good morning)
Kwanto foahee (Good morning to you.Usually this salute is given by an elder to a younger or people of the same age.Young people can not give this to their elders).
Kwanto maa/babaa/Kyekya/Kyekuoo/kaaka/daada
Meaning-Good   · morning   mother /father/grandfather/grandmother/brother/sister.

Reply- (Nanto=Goodmorning)
Nanto maa/babaa/Kyekya/Kyekuoo/kaaka/dada Or Aika
Nkeeku/Mbe/Mae/Kaaka/Daada
Mweanto foahee vade (Good morning youths) .
Mweanto foahee Dinama (Goodmorning people;men and
women)
Mweanto foahee vamaa (Good morning mothers)
After noon greatings
Kosida   fo   hayee
maa/babaa/Kyekya/Kyekuoo/kaaka/daada
Reply   1-(I'm   pretty   good)=   Nifokisha   dua
maa/babaa/Kyekya/Kyekuoo/kaaka/daada
How are you also ? =Bontafoo ?
Reply 2-(I'm very good)=Nshisha deny'n
Thanks (Mentioned as gender or family name) =Aika
Nkeeku/Mbe/Mae/Maimu/Mmari
How are you?
Kyifoaye huyee? Reply-(I'm good= Nifokishaa)
Congratulation for a good work
Korolya maa, babaa, Kyekya, Kyekuoo, kaaka, dada
Aika Nkeeku/Mbe/Mae
How have you been?.Usually for people of the same age or
an elder greeting the younger person.
Bontafoo maa, babaa, Kyekya, Kyekuoo, kaaka, dada
Aika Nkeeku/Mbe/Mae
Nifokishaa

KIMOCHI
Morning greeting
Kuamtso mbe/mae/mbe/mai/wawae=Good morning fa-
ther/mother/grandfather/grandmother/brother or sister
Reply- Kapfo naiyo manako meaning And you too my

child

Afternoon greeting

Mbonyi tse tsinda mbe/mae/mbe/mai/wawae =Good afternoon fa-ther/mother/grandfather/grandmother/brother or sister

Reply-tsitsicha mbe/mae/mbe/mai/wawae

Omtana mbe/mae/mbe/mai/wawae =Congratulation for good work fa-ther/mother/grandfather/grandmother/brother or sister

Reply- Haika mbe/mae/mbe/mai/wawae.For a child use manako

How are you?

Shimbonyi

Shimbonyi Shapfo

Shimbonyi sha ngamenyi.-meaning Good morning.

Shimbonyi sha ndeo /mayo/ sahuyo/kyekuyo/wawayo/mananu –meaning how is your father/mother/grandfather/grandmother/ elder brother or sister/young brother or sister (Usually this salute is given by an elder to a younger or people of the same age. Young people can not give this to their elders).

Reply1 –Shishicha kapisa, Haika, ungiwie shapfo.

Reply 2-Njiimcha kapisa

 Night greeting

Laakucha mbe/mae/mbe/mai/wawae

Reply- Laakucha mbe/mae/mbe/mai/wawae

NB: In Mochi Morning is ngamenyi, afternoon is mfiri ,evening is kyiukanyi and night is kyio.

COUNTING IN CHAGGAS

No.	KIMORANG'U	KIHOROMBO	MACHAME	KIWOSO	SHIRA	URU	KIMOCHI
1	Kim	Imu	Imwi	Imu	Kimwi	Imu	IM
2	Shiwi	Iwili	Iwi	Ivi	Fivili	Viwi	Shiwi
3	Shiraru	Isadu	Isaru	Isadu	Fihahu	Vilalu	Shiraru
4	Shiina	Inyaa	Inya	Iinya	Fiine	Viina	Shiina
5	Shitanu	Stanu	Isanu	Tanu	Fihanu	Vitanu	Shitanu
6	Shirandaru	Sita	Sita	Sita	Firdahu	Sita	Shirandaru
7	Mvungare	Saba	Saba	Saba	Mfungahe	Isaba	Mfungade
8	Nyanya	Nane	Nyanya	Nane	Nyanyi	Inane	Nyanya
9	Kenda	Kenda	Kenda	Tisa	Kyeda	Itisa	Kenda
10	Ikumi	Ikumi	Ikumi	Ikumi	Ikumi	Iku	Ikumi

					mi	

Naming power of tens

Digit	Chagga	English	Digit #
1	Imu	One	1
10	Ikumi	Tens	2
100	Iyana (Iana)	Hundreds	3
1000	Kiku(Shiku)	Thousands	4

Uncountable items were typically measured by the volume of their standard containers. Chagga accurately counts the uncountable items as one personal arm (Kkoko ki-mu), two arms (Maoko awili), one bowl (Bakuli imu) or one basket (Kkabu ki-mu). They count correctly, multiple digits by group-ing.

Twelve is ten and two (Ikumi na iwili), thirty is three tens (Makumi aladu), fifty-two is five tens and two (makumi Atanu na iwili).

Glossary

Definitions and Chagge examples

Culture represents shared norms, values, taboos, myth, rituals, beliefs, customs and traditions of a group that typically define and guide appropriate and inappropriate attitudes and behaviors.

With respect to Chaggas, the ancestors formed a culture on the roots of morals and ethics sharped into patterns of behavior for the members of the society to mollify the social harmony and cooperative living, justice and fairness. Moral and ethics give insight into the philosophical thinking or ideas and practice of the society.

Philosophical thinking derived the word Moral from a Greek word "Mos" which means custom and therefore morals are the customs established by a group of individuals. Chagga morals include, but are not limited to; do not cheat, greet the elders, be obedient, be on time, be loyal, be patient, it is bad to steal and it is good to help each other. Elders emphasized morals in customary life of the Chagga.

In the same way, we derive ethics from a Greek word "Ethikos" which means character. Whereas we define the character of a group of the society as the concepts, principles, satisfaction, social relations and attitudes held by the members of the society about what is right or wrong. Chagga's eth-ics includes but not limited to honesty, kindness, empathy, determination and perseverance, generosity, respect, organization, knowledge and wisdom. Mangi supremacy reinforced the ethics during religious ceremonies, judiciary and parliamentary sessions.

Value is a social character that deserves; the importance, worth, or usefulness and a norm is something that is usual, typical, or standard.

A custom is a repeated action that has become typical of a group and which parents or elders of a group hand it down. A tradition is a custom that has become common-ly repeated and continues down the line because of historically learned behaviors. Example of Chagga traditions are; eating meat, drinking of blood, worship ancestors, compartment houses, eating and drinking banana products, fantabulous marriages and distinct funeral services.

A taboo is a social or religious custom of prohibiting or restricting a particular practice or forbidding association with a particular person, place, or thing. There are Chagga taboos~ food, sex, menstrual and pregnancy.

A myth is a traditional story, especially one concerning the previous history of a people or explaining a natural or social phenomenon, and typically involving super-natural beings or events. There is a Chagga myth of moving around a modidi tree to cure mumps.

A rite (ivika mtete) is a prescribed form or manner governing the words or actions for a ceremony, and a ritual (mtete) is the ceremony comprising a series of actions per-formed according to a prescribed order. Chagga ritual~during marriage, a new born and death ceremonies.

A belief is a conviction or acceptance that certain things are true or real with no proof. Chagga believes ~ on God

(Ruwa) and ancestor spirits.

The Chagga culture inculcates human values that make up the primary—perhaps the fundamental— criteria that not solely inspire but also justify bodily actions that affect other human beings. Chagga culture a point of departure, for the interpersonal interactions that offer an insight on how to share, take turns and compromise with other individuals. The centrality of the socialization helps to develop and define our thoughts, feelings, and actions, and it provides us with a model for behaviors, which are inspired by the Chagga people. The corner point of the socialization of the Chaggas is their language. The humanistic foundations and features of Chagga culture are extensively discussed to examine its evolution from the previous experiences to the current impressions following colonial invasion, African politics and technological developments, economic and ecological changes.

A clan is a group of 100 or less house holds of related families

Bibliography

Hemp A, 1999, "An ethnobotanical study of Mt. Kilimanjaro", Ecotropica 5: 147-165.

Mhando, D. G. and G. Mbeyale 2010., "An Analysis of the Coffee Value Chains in the Kilimanjaro Region, Tanzania ". NCCR North-South Dialogue, 27. Online. http://www.north-south.ch/publications/Infosystem/On-line%20Dokumente/Upload/Mhando& Mbeyale_NCCR_Dialogue_27_2010.pdf (Accessed April 20, 2023).

Dundas C, 1968, "Kilimanjaro and Its People: A History of Wachagga, their Laws, Customs and Legends", Together with Some (1st ed.). Routledge. https://doi.org/10.4324/9780203042144

Maanga G.S, 2015, "Rewriting Chagga History: Focus on Ethno-Anthropological Distortions and Misconceptions". Global Journal of Human-Social Science Research, 15.

Stahl, Kathleen Mary,1964 "History of the Chagga People of Kilimanjaro", London: Mouton

Raymond S. Mosha, 2013 "Spirituality Directions and African Directions Spirituality", The Way, 52/3 (July 2013), 105–114. Accessed online. https://www .theway.org.UK on 21/04/2023

John S. Mbiti, 1999, "African Religions and Philosophy" Nairobi, Heinemann, 1969, 106.

Gutmann Bruno Ilona Gruber Drivdal and Shelby Tucker. 2017. "Poetry and Thinking of the Chagga: Contributions to East African Ethnology." Oxford: Signal Books Limited

Petro Itoshi Marealle, 2002, "Maisha ya Mchagga Hapa Duniani na Ahera", Dar es Salaam: Mkuki na Nyota, 29 Dec 2002,

Bender, M. V. (2008). Holy Ghost in the Highlands: The Spiritans on Kilimanjaro, 1892-1953. Spiritan Horizons, 3 (3). Retrieved from https://dsc.duq.edu/spiritan-horizons/vol3/iss3/12

Elders, Machame, Uru, Old Moshi, Siha, Kibosho, Kiruwa, Marangu, Rombo Interview by Humphrey Mselle. August to October 2018. OH# 30, Oral History Project, Kilimanjaro

Elders, Donald Malyango, Selestine Kitema, Interview by Dennis Lyakurwa. December 2018. OH# 33, Oral History Project, Kilimanjaro